What is Language?

SonLight Education Ministry
United States of America

A Suggested Daily Schedule

(Adapt this schedule to your family needs.)

5:00 a.m.   Arise–Personal Worship

6:00 a.m.   Family Worship and Bible Class–With Father

7:00 a.m.   Breakfast

8:00 a.m.   Practical Arts*–Domestic Activities
                              Agriculture
                              Industrial Arts
                              (especially those related to
                              the School Lessons)

10:00 a.m.   School Lessons
                  (Take a break for some physical exercise
                  during this time slot.)

12:00 p.m.   Dinner Preparations
                  (Health class could be included at this time
                  or a continued story.)

1:00 p.m.   Dinner

2:00 p.m.   Practical Arts* or Fine Arts
                  (Music and Crafts)
                  (especially those related to
                  the School Lessons)

5:00 p.m.   Supper

6:00 p.m.   Family Worship–Father
                  (Could do History Class)

7:00 p.m.   Personal time with God–Bed Preparation

8:00 p.m.   Bed

*Daily nature walk can be in morning or afternoon.

The Desire of All Nations

This book is a part of a curriculum that is built upon the life of Christ entitled, "The Desire of All Nations," for grades 2-8. Any of the books in this curriculum can be used by themselves or as an entire program.

INFORMATION ABOUT THE 2-8 GRADE PROGRAM

Multi-level

This program is written on a multi-level. That means that each booklet has material for grades 2-8. This is so the whole family in these grades may work from the same books. It is difficult for a busy mother to have 2 or more children and each have a different set of books. Remember, the Bible is written for all ages.

The Bible—the Primary Textbook

The books in this program are designed to teach the parent and the student how to learn academic subjects by using the Bible as a primary textbook.

The Desire of Ages

The Desire of Ages by Ellen G. White is used as a textbook to go with the Bible. This focuses on the early life of Christ, when He was a child. Children relate best to Christ as a child and youth.

Lesson Numbers

The big number in the top right corner on the cover of this book is the Lesson Number and corresponds with the chapter number in the book *The Desire of Ages*. For example, Lesson 1 in the school program will go along with chapter 1 in *The Desire of Ages*. Usually each family starts at the beginning with Lesson 1. Most children have not had a true Bible program, therefore they need the foundation built. If there is academic material that they have already covered, they do the Bible part and review then pass quickly on.

Seven Academic Subjects

There are seven academic subjects in this program—Health, Mathematics, Music, Science–Nature, History/Geography/Prophecy, Language, Voice–Speech.

Language Program

A good, solid language program is recommended to be used along with the SonLight materials.

The Riggs Institute has a multi-sensory teaching method that accommodates every child's unique learning style. Their program is called *Writing and Spelling Road to Reading and Thinking*. Order by calling (800) 200-4840 or visit www.riggsinst.org. (Disclaimer: SonLight does not endorse the reading books recommended in the Riggs' program.)

Another option which you might find more user friendly and is similar to the Riggs program but from a Christian perspective is *Spell to Write and Read* by Wanda Sanseri. To order, call Wanda Sanseri at (503) 654-2300 or visit https://www.bhibooks.net/swr.html

"God With Us"
Lesson 1 – Love

The following books are those you will need for this lesson.
All of these can be obtained from www.sonlighteducation.com

The Rainbow Covenant – Study the spiritual meaning of colors and make your own rainbow book.

Health
What is Health?

Math
What is Mathematics?

Music
What is Music?

Science/Nature
What is Nature?

A Casket – Coloring book and story. Learn how to treat the gems of the Bible.

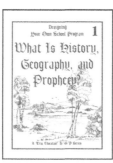

H/G/P
What is History, Geography and Prophecy?

Language
What is Language?

Speech/Voice
What is the Voice?

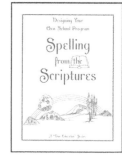

Spelling from the Scriptures

Bible Study – Learn how to study the Bible and helpful use tools.

Bible
The Desire of all Nations I
Teacher Study Guide

Student Study Guide

Bible Lesson Study Guide

Memory Verses
The Desire of all Nations I
Scripture Songs Book
and MP3 files

Our Nature Study Book – Your personal nature journal.

Outline of "The Desire of all Nations" Lesson 1

Bible	Health	Math	Music	Nature	H/G/P	Language	Voice

READ THIS BEFORE BEGINNING

Cover the Teacher's Section of each school book before beginning that subject.

It is best to cover only a few concepts at once and understand them well and not run a marathon with a young person's mind. If this outline moves too fast for you SLOW down. Teach one idea and teach it well!

This school program is not a race with time, rather it is an experience with God.

The parents are to represent their Father in Heaven before the children—students.

Together learn about the Character Qualities and help one another in a godly manner to reach the finish line together.

Week 1 — Month 1
Lesson 1
Day 1

Bible: Family Morning Worship *Covenant Notebook* (1) Music, Prayer, MV (2) Read pages 1-2 in the "Covenant Notebook" and discuss. (3) Sometime during the day take a nature walk looking for rainbows. (4) Begin finding pictures of complete rainbows to put into the plastic sheets behind the "Rainbows" page. Read and discuss the "Rainbows" page.

Health: Use these songs during this week, "All Things Bright & Beautiful," "This is My Father's World," and "We Shall Know." Find this music in *Christ in Song* book which is included in these materials under the title "Song Books."

Day 2

Bible: (1) Music, Prayer, MV (2) Read page 3 in the "Covenant Notebook" and discuss. (Also use page 7)

Health: Lay out Lesson 1 of the School Program showing the the front covers of each book, *What is Health?, What is Mathematics?, What is Music?, What is Nature?,*

Math: *What is H/G/P?, What is Language?, and What is Voice?.* Each book will have a color cover of one of the colors of the rainbow. Place them in order as the rainbow colors

---

INSTRUCTIONS

Music: deomonstrate in a picture. Refer to page 7 of the *Covenant Notebook* to see what each color means and how it relates to the subject that bears that color.

Nature: (Examples: Health = Christ sacrificed His body on the cross for you. Mathematics = Deals in numbers saved and lost.

H/G/P: Music = Right music can turn our thoughts from things of this world to Divinity. Nature = Right growth in character.

Language: H/G/P = The history of obedience and disobedience; geography of lands where the gospel is to be spread; prophecy telling us the future of those keeping the law.

Voice: Language and Voice = How God's royal people should write, speak, and act to prepare for His kingdom.

Bible	Health	Math	Music	Nature	H/G/P	Language	Voice

(3) Sometime during the day take a nature walk looking for rainbows.

(4) Begin finding pictures of complete rainbows to put into the plastic sheets behind the "Rainbows" page. Read and discuss the "Rainbows" page.

Day 3-4

(1) Music, Prayer, MV

(2) Read pages 4-9 in the "Covenant Notebook" and discuss.

(3) Sometime during the day take a nature walk looking for white items (or the color pages).

(4) Begin finding pictures of white things in nature to put into the plastic sheets behind the "White" page. Read and discuss the "White" page.

Day 5

Review what you have learned.

INSTRUCTIONS

Once the white page is completed then move on to the red page and so forth, always finding things from nature for your pictures. And on your nature walks fine the color you are currently working on. Do not look for man made things! Before going on the nature walk each day, read and discuss the information in the color section.

After day 5, and reviewing only what you have learned to that point, plan only to work on the *Covenant Notebook* one day a week until that book is finished (Use time in the afternoon and not during the regular school hours). However, do not forget to review the *Covenant Notebook* when you deem it necessary, and if you should find a new picture for it, stop and put it into *Covenant Notebook*. It gives you an opportunity to review lessons with the children.

Lesson 12 of Nature in this series is about the rainbow and would be a wonderful time to make a recommitment to God.

This *Covenant Notebook* is to prepare you for the 2-8 School Lessons. On week 2 begin the School Lessons.

Bible	Health	Math	Music	Nature	H/G/P	Language	Voice

Week 2 Lesson 1

START THE 2-8 PROGRAM, "The Desire Of All Nations."

Bible — Day 1
"God With Us"
(1) Music
("O Come, O come, Immanuel,"
"I Love Thee,"
"Thou didst Leave Thy Throne"),
Prayer,
MV (Mt 1:21)
(2) Read and discuss Ge 3:14-15; 12:1-3.
Discuss the Character Quality.

Health — Day 1
What Is Health?
(1) Open Bibles and read II Sa 20:9.
(2) Read or tell information.
Do pages 1-17 or what you can cover. Discuss.

Math — Day 1
What Is Math...?
(1) Open Bibles and read Mt 11:29.
(2) Read or tell information.
Do pages 1-8 or what you can cover. Discuss.

Language — Day 1
Writing and Spelling Road to Reading and Thinking (WSRRT) (1) Do your daily assignments for *WSRRT*.

If you are still working on this program continue until you finish at least the 2nd teacher's notebook.

INSTRUCTIONS

If you are still using the *Family Bible Lessons* do them for one of your worships each day and use *The Desire of all Nations* for the other worship each day.

These are the items you will need for worship for *The Desire of all Nations* Bible program: Old King James Bible (NOT the New King James Bible)
"*The Desire of all Nations*," Volume 1, Study Guide for the KJV Bible Lessons
The Desire of all Nations Teacher and Student Study Guides #1 (Chapters from *The Desire of Ages* Bible text book)
The Desire of all Nations Song Book #1 and CD Music #1 for Memory Verses
Christ in Song Song Book #1, 2, 3, 4

These are the items you will need for class time:

What is Health?; *What is Mathematics?*; *What is Music?*; *What is Nature?*; *What is H/G/P?*; *What is Language?*; and *What is Voice?*.
Our Nature Study Book "The Casket" Story & Coloring Book
Bible Study
Road Map and Route Catalogue

Bible	Health	Math	Music	Nature	H/G/P	Language	Voice
Day 2 "God With Us" (1) Music ("O Come, O come, Immanuel," "I Love Thee," "Thou didst Leave Thy Throne"), Prayer, MV (Mt 1:21; Jn 8:28) (2) Read and discuss Gal 3:16; Ge 49:10; De 18:17-19; II Sam 7:12-17.	**Day 2** *What Is Health?* (1) Open Bibles and read I Co 12:23. (2) Read or tell information. Do pages 18-26 or what you can cover. Discuss.	**Day 2** *What Is Math...?* (1) Open Bibles and read Luke 6:38; Is 40:12; Ps 147:4; Is 40:26; Job 28:25. (2) Read or tell information. Do pages 9-22 or what you can cover. Discuss. **END**				**Day 2** *Writing and Spelling Road to Reading and Thinking* (1) Do your daily assignments for *WSRRT*.	
Day 3 "God With Us" (1) Music, Prayer, MV (Mt 1:21; Jn 8:28) (2) Read and discuss Ez 21:25-27; Lu 1:32; Isa 9:6-7.	**Day 3** *What Is Health?* (1) Open Bibles and read Pr 26:2. (2) Read or tell information. Do pages 27-35 or what you can cover. Discuss.		**Day 3** *What Is Music?* (1) Open Bibles and read Zeph 3:17. (2) Read or tell information. Do pages 1-6 or what you can cover. Discuss.			**Day 3** *Writing and Spelling Road to Reading and Thinking* (1) Do your daily assignments for *WSRRT*.	
Day 4 "God With Us" (1) Review what you have already covered.	**Day 4** *What Is Health?* (1) Review pages 1-35.	**Day 4** *What Is Math...?* (1) Review.	**Day 4** *What Is Music?* (1) Open Bibles and read Re 14:2-3. (2) Read or tell information. Do pages 7-17 or what you can cover. Discuss.			**Day 4** *Writing and Spelling Road to Reading and Thinking* (1) Do your daily assignments for *WSRRT*.	
Day 5	**Day 5**	**Day 5**	**Day 5**			**Day 5** Review	

Find practical applications from your textbooks you have thus far used this week. You will find them listed under "**Reinforce**." Choose and use today.

Bible	Health	Math	Music	Nature	H/G/P	Language	Voice
Week 3 **Lesson 1** **Day 1** "God With Us" (1) Music, Prayer, MV (Mt 1:21; Jn 8:28) (2) Read and discuss Ps 45:1-8; 72:1-11; Is 53.	**Day 1** *What Is Health?* (1) Open Bibles and read James 5:14. (2) Read or tell information. Do pages 36-39 or what you can cover. Discuss.		**Day 1** *What Is Music?* (1) Open Bibles and read I Ki 19:12. (2) Read or tell information. Do pages 18-30 or what you can cover. Discuss.			**Day 1** *Writing and Spelling Road to Reading and Thinking* (1) Do your daily assignments for *WSRRT*.	
Day 2 "God With Us" (1) Music, Prayer, MV (Mt 1:21; Jn 8:28; Jn 8:50) (2) Read and discuss Zec 12:10; Jn 14:9; Mt 1:23; Jn 1:1-4.	**Day 2** *What Is Health?* (1) Open Bibles and read De 34:7. (2) Read or tell information. Do pages 40-44 or what you can cover. Discuss.		**Day 2** *What Is Music?* (1) Open Bibles and read I Chr 13:8. (2) Read or tell information. Do pages 31-52 or what you can cover. Discuss. END			**Day 2** *Writing and Spelling Road to Reading and Thinking* (1) Do your daily assignments for *WSRRT*.	
Day 3 "God With Us" (1) Music, Prayer, MV (Mt 1:21; Jn 8:28; Jn 8:50; Phil 2:5-11) (2) Read and discuss *The Desire of Ages* 19-20:0.	**Day 3** *What Is Health?* (1) Open Bibles and read Ez 33:11. (2) Read or tell information. Do pages 45-53 or what you can cover. Discuss.			**Day 3** *What Is Nature?* (1) Open Bibles and read Ro 13:10. (2) Read or tell information. Do pages 1-11 or what you can cover. Discuss.		**Day 3** *Writing and Spelling Road to Reading and Thinking* (1) Do your daily assignments for *WSRRT*.	

Bible	Health	Math	Music	Nature	H/G/P	Language	Voice
Day 4 "God With Us" (1) Music, Prayer, MV (Mt 1:21; Jn 8:28; Jn 8:50; Phil 2:5-11) (2) Read and discuss *The Desire of Ages* 20:2-21:0.	**Day 4** *What Is Health?* (1) Open Bibles and read De 7:15; De 32:46; and Pr 4:20, 22. (2) Read or tell information. Do pages 54-60 or what you can cover. Discuss.			**Day 4** *What Is Nature?* (1) Open Bibles and read Ps 40:5; Ps 111:4. (2) Read or tell information. Do pages 12-17 or what you can cover. Discuss.		**Day 4** *Writing and Spelling Road to Reading and Thinking* (1) Do your daily assignments for *WSRRT*.	
Day 5 "God With Us" (1) Review.	**Day 5** *What Is Health?* (1) Review pages 1-60.	**Day 5** *What Is Math...?* (1) Review.	**Day 5** *What Is Music?* (1) Review.	**Day 5** *What Is Nature?* (1) Review pages 1-17.		**Day 5** *Writing and Spelling Road to Reading and Thinking* (1) Do your daily assignments for *WSRRT*.	
Week 4 **Lesson 1**							
Day 1 "God With Us" (1) Music, Prayer, MV (Mt 1:21; Jn 8:28; Jn 8:50; Phil 2:5-11) (2) Read and discuss *The Desire of Ages* 21:1-2.	**Day 1** *What Is Health?* (1) Open Bibles and read De 7:15; De 32:46; and Pr 4:20, 22. (2) Read the story. Do pages 61-80. Discuss.			**Day 1** *What Is Nature?* (1) Open Bibles and read Job 12:7-8. (2) Read or tell information. Do pages 18-23 or what you can cover. Discuss.		**Day 1** *Writing and Spelling Road to Reading and Thinking* (1) Do your daily assignments for *WSRRT*.	
Day 2 "God With Us" (1) Music, Prayer, MV (Mt 1:21; Jn 8:28; Jn 8:50; Phil 2:5-11) (2) Read and discuss *The Desire of Ages* 21:3-22:1.	**Day 2** *What Is Health* (1) Open Bibles and review De 7:15; De 32:46; and Pr 4:20, 22. (2) Do pages 81-86. Discuss. END			**Day 2** *What Is Nature?* (1) Open Bibles and read Ps 143:5. (2) Read or tell information. Do pages 24-30 or what you can cover. END		**Day 2** *WSRRT* (1) Do your daily assignments for *WSRRT*. Continue the *WSRRT* but add the Language lessons in whenever it is time to do them. **This will not be repeated.**	

Bible	Health	Math	Music	Nature	H/G/P	Language	Voice
Day 3 "God With Us" (1) Music, Prayer, MV (Mt 1:21; Jn 8:28; Jn 8:50; Phil 2:5-11) (2) Read and discuss *The Desire of Ages* 21:3-22:3.					**Day 3** *What Is H/G/P?* (1) Open Bibles and read He 1:10. (2) Read or tell information. Do pages 1-6 or what you can cover. Discuss. Choose a good mission book to begin reading as a family.	**Day 3** *What Is Language?* (1) Open Bibles and read Col 3:16. (2) Read or tell information. Do pages 1-10 or what you can cover + *WSRRT*. Discuss.	
Day 4 "God With Us" (1) Music, Prayer, MV (Mt 1:21; Jn 8:28; Jn 8:50; Phil 2:5-11) (2) Read and discuss *The Desire of Ages* 22:4-24:1.					**Day 4** *What Is H/G/P?* (1) Open Bibles and read Ps 119:105 & He 13:1. (2) Read or tell information. Do pages 7-14. Discuss.	**Day 4** *What Is Language?* (1) Open Bibles and read Pr 25:11. (2) Read or tell information. Do pages 11-17 + *WSRRT*. Discuss.	**Day 4** *What Is Voice?* (1) Open Bibles and read Ps 105:2. (2) Read or tell information. Do pages 1-4. Discuss.
Day 5 "God With Us" (1) Review. (2) Read and discuss *The Desire of Ages* 24:2-26:3.	**Day 5** *What Is Health?* (1) Review	**Day 5** *What Is Math...?* (1) Review.	**Day 5** *What Is Music?* (1) Review.	**Day 5** *What Is Nature?* (1) Review.	**Day 5** *What Is H/G/P?* (1) Review pages 1-14.	**Day 5** *What Is Language?* (1) Review pages 1-17.	**Day 5** *What Is Voice?* (1) Review pages 1-4.

Week 1 (5) | Month 2 |
Lesson 1

Bible	Health	Math	Music	Nature	H/G/P	Language	Voice
Day 1 "God With Us" (1) Music, Prayer, MV. (2) Read and discuss *The Desire of Ages* 24:2-26:3.					**Day 1** *What Is H/G/P?* (1) Open Bibles and read Jer 10:12. (2) Read or tell information. Do pages 15-25Aa or what you can cover. Discuss.	**Day 1** *What Is Language?* (1) Open Bibles and read Jn 1:1. (2) Read or tell information. Do pages 18-22 or what you can cover. Discuss. **END**	**Day 1** *What Is Voice?* (1) Open Bibles and read Ps 32:2. (2) Read or tell information. Do pages 5-8. Discuss. **END**

> Do your daily assignments for *WSRRT*.

> If there is any information that the student should know and does not—REVIEW.

Bible	Health	Math	Music	Nature	H/G/P	Language	Voice
Day 2 "God With Us" (1) Music, Prayer, MV. (2) Expand or review any part of the lesson. (Could use section about William Miller in H/G/P.) **Day 3** "God With Us" (1) Music, Prayer, MV. (2) Expand or review any part of the lesson. (Could use the section in H/G/P. "The Schools of the Prophets.") **Day 4** "God With Us" (1) Music, Prayer, MV. (2) Expand or review any part of the lesson. (Could explain why the Apocrypha books are not included in Bible.) **END**					**Day 2** *What Is H/G/P?* (1) Open Bibles and read II Pe 1:21. (2) Read or tell information. Do pages 26-47 or what you can cover. Discuss. (Story about "William Miller" may take longer.) **Day 3** *What Is H/G/P?* (1) Open Bibles and read Ja 3:17 & Pr 9:10. (2) Read or tell information. Do pages 48-65 or what you can cover. Discuss. **Day 4** *What Is H/G/P?* (1) Open Bibles and read Ex 17:14 & Ge 5:22. (2) Read or tell information. Do pages 66-78 or what you can cover. Discuss. **END**	**Day 2** *Writing and Spelling Road to Reading and Thinking* (1) Do your daily assignments for *WSRRT.* **Day 3** *Writing and Spelling Road to Reading and Thinking* (1) Do your daily assignments for *WSRRT.* **Day 4** *Writing and Spelling Road to Reading and Thinking* (1) Do your daily assignments for *WSRRT.*	**Day 2** *What Is Voice?* (1) Review **Day 4-5** Use this time to review anything from lesson 1.

On day 5 review any subject in Lesson 1 that needs a better understanding.

Week 2 | **Month 2**

Lesson 2

Day 1 "The Chosen People" (1) Music, Prayer, MV. (2) Read and discuss.

Continue the process with Lesson 2. See the *Road Map and Route Catalogue.*

Language Instructions

1. **Grades 1-4** – *Writing and Spelling Road to Reading and Thinking* (or also called *The Writing Road to Reading*)

This program presents a step-by-step rationale and instructional procedure for teaching a four-year, fully integrated language arts method, concurrently, with visual, auditory, verbal, and motor cognitive developmental skills. We have found it easy to use and a superior program. With grades 1 you will use book 1, with grade 2 you will use book 2 (year 2), book 3 (year 3), and year four review and work on any weak areas. During grades 2-4 you will include the use of the SonLight language program. See the "Road Map and Route."

Order the books from "The Riggs Institute." Go to the web to find their current phone number. Order the following:

• *Writing and Spelling Road to Reading and Thinking* – Level 1 (grade 1)
• *Writing and Spelling Road to Reading and Thinking* – Level 2 (grade 2)
• *Writing and Spelling Road to Reading and Thinking* – Level 3 (grade 3)
(You must start with this program as you cannot start at Level 2)
• Flash Cards
• Phonogram Sounds CD

2. See the sheet "Additional Spelling Words."

3. Teaching the SonLight lessons:
(A) Read the Teachers Section
(B) Begin the Student Section
(C) Read the General Title and Bible text, discuss the Bible text and its meaning.
(D) Teacher and student take turns reading or teacher explains the information.
(E) Read and discuss the information enclosed in boxes sometimes as Reflect or Remarkable Facts.
(F) Do all the Reinforce and Reminds as these are the practicals.
(G) Do the Reviews as written or verbal.

4. If you have any questions contact SonLight at (509) 684-6843.

Additional Spelling Words

These words will not be listed in your school books. Use this sheet.

Lesson	Words	
	Place I - II	**Place III**
2	Matthew Mark Luke John	Genesis Exodus Leviticus Numbers Deuteronomy
3	Acts Romans I Corinthians II Corinthians	Joshua Judges Ruth I Samuel II Samuel
4	Galatians Ephesians Philippians Colossians	I Kings II Kings I Chronicles II Chronicles Ezra
5	I Thessalonians II Thessalonians I Timothy II Timothy	Nehemiah Esther Job Psalm Proverbs
6	Titus Philemon Hebrews James	Ecclesiastes Song of Solomon (Canticles) Isaiah Jeremiah

Lesson	Words	
	Place I - II	Place III
7	I Peter II Peter I John II John III John	Lamentations Ezekiel Daniel Hosea Joel
8	Jude Revelation	Amos Obadiah Jonah Micah Nahum
9	Review	Habakkuk Zephaniah Haggai Zechariah Malachi
10	Review	Review

Book of Remembrance

At the end of each day, request that the child make a record of how the Lord blessed him during that day. This record will be called "The Book of Remembrance" and it should be written in a special notebook. Just as heaven is keeping a record of the good deeds of the children of God (Malachi 3:16), so let the youth keep a record of the good deeds of the Lord in their behalf. We are told: "Let such ones keep a diary, and when the Lord gives them an interesting experience, let them write it down, as Samuel did when the armies of Israel won a victory over the Philistines. He set up a monument of thankfulness, saying, *'Hitherto hath the Lord helped us.'* Brethren, where are the monuments by which you keep in view the **love** and goodness of God? Strive to keep fresh in your minds the help that the Lord has given you in your efforts to help others...every fear that has been expelled, every mercy shown—trace a record of it in your diary." (*2 Bible Commentary* 1012)

"O Lord, have we waited for thee; the desire of our soul is to thy name, and the remembrance of thee" (Isaiah 26:8).

For the children, this will mean they will need to review the day and trace how the Lord has helped them personally. It may be that He has helped them to gain a new spiritual insight through some object lesson they learned.

By this good practice of keeping a "Book of Remembrance," several things will be accomplished.

1. The child will develop the habit of looking for the personal touch of God in his life and will in the process gather up the fragments of many small blessings that might otherwise be lost.

2. A daily reflection will help to more permanently store the knowledge gained. "We have nothing to fear for the future, except as we shall forget the way the Lord has led us, and His teaching in our past history." (*Life Sketches* 196)

3. Skill will be gained in well-ordered thinking and composition.

"Remember his marvellous works that he hath done, his wonders, and the judgments of his mouth" (I Chronicles 16:12).

"Then they that feared the Lord spake often one to another: and the Lord hearkened, and heard it, and a book of remembrance was written before him for them that feared the Lord, and that thought upon his name" (Malachi 3:16).

"And thou shalt remember all the way which the Lord thy God led thee..." (Deuteronomy 8:2).

"I will remember the years of the right hand of the Most High. I will remember the works of the Lord: surely I will remember thy wonders of old" (Psalm 77:10-11).

More Instructions

1. Reading class comes during Bible class—with the Bible as the primary reader and other reading material indicated for each subject. For extra reading books, read mission stories and histories of godly, great people.

2. If the student is having reading problems take him through the "First Grade Reader." This booklet is the first eight chapters of Genesis with comprehension questions. Follow the directions in that booklet.

3. Usually if there are extra material for the Bible Class it is found in the teacher's section of the Language lesson.

4. When you have a section in Language that is too old for Level I, let the child practice printing his memory verse, reviewing his spelling words, and other information from his lessons. He could also review some of his spelling rules taken from *Spelling From the Scriptures.*

Bible Class Instructions

• Below you will find extra material to use with your Bible class. Never move ahead of the Bible Lesson or chapter from *The Desire of Ages* until you have completed the academics for that particular lesson. This is why we sometimes provide you with extra lesson material when the Bible Lesson is short.

• If you do finish the Bible Lessons before you complete that academic subjects that go with that particular lesson and also use the extra material then use the Nature Lesson for Bible Class.

Further Bible material for Lesson 2 "God's Chosen People."

Bible verses to study:
    Isaiah 27:6
    Isaiah 60:1-3

Prophets and Kings, Pages 703-721
    "The House of Israel"

Bible verses to study:
    Isaiah 56:7
    Isaiah 5:3-7
    Ezekiel 34:4

The Acts of the Apostles, pages 9-16, "God's Purposes for His Church"

If all you cover is one verse, or one or two paragraphs in each lesson, that is fine, as long as the child understands what the material means. Go SLOW, explain well.

"Teach ONE idea and teach it well."

• You might like to have the student draw illustrations of the lesson.

• Use a large Bible map and follow Jesus as He walked on this earth.

• If there is younger members of the family use the large Bible in Felt set and let them each week make up the picture of the lesson.

Each week we pray for each family who has contacted us for materials. Please remember us in your prayers.

"Wherefore also we pray always for you, that our God would count you worthy of this calling, and fulfil all the good pleasure of his goodness, and the work of faith with power" (II Thessalonians 1:11).

Table of Contents

Little Acts of Love

Not mighty deeds make up the sun
    Of happiness below;
But little acts of kindliness,
    Which any child may show.

A glass of water timely brought,
    An offered easy chair,
A turning of the window-blind,
    That all may feel the air.

An early flower, unasked, bestowed,
    A light and cautious tread,
A voice, to gentlest whisper hushed,
    To spare the aching head.

Oh! deeds like these, though little things,
    Yet purest **love** disclose,
As fragrant atoms in the air
    Reveal the hidden rose.

Outwitted

He drew a circle and shut me out—
Heretic, rebel, a thing to flout.
But **love** and I had the wit to win:
We drew a circle that took him in.
    —Edwin Markham

Teacher
Section

"A word fitly spoken
is like apples of gold
in pictures of silver."
Proverbs 25:11

INSTRUCTIONS
For the Teacher

Step 1

Study the Bible Lesson and begin to memorize the Memory Verses. Familiarize Yourself With the Character Quality. The student can answer the Bible Review Questions. See page 6. Use the Steps in Bible Study.

Bible Lesson

"God With Us" – Genesis 3:14-15; 12:1-3; Galatians 3:16; Genesis 49:10; Deuteronomy 18:17-19; II Samuel 7:12-17; Ezekiel 21:25-27; Luke 1:32; Isaiah 9:6-7; Psalm 45:1-8; 72:1-11; Isaiah 53; Zechariah 12:10; John 14:9; John 1:1-4; Matthew 1:23

Memory Verses

Matthew 1:23; Matthew 1:20-21; John 8:28; 6:57; 7:18; 8:50; Philippians 2:5-11

Character Quality

Love – an affection of the mind excited by beauty and worth of any kind, or by the qualities of an object; charity.

Antonyms – hate; detestableness; abomination; loathing; scorn; disdainfulness; selfishness

Character Quality Verse

I Corinthians 13:4-7 – *"Charity suffereth long, and is kind; charity envieth not; charity vaunteth not itself, is not puffed up,*

"Doth not behave itself unseemly, seeketh not her own, is not easily provoked, thinketh no evil;

"Rejoiceth not in iniquity, but rejoiceth in the truth;

"Beareth all things, believeth all things, hopeth all things, endureth all things."

Step 2

Understand How To/ And

A. Do the Spelling Cards so the student can begin to build his own spiritual dictionary.

B. Mark Your Bible.

C. Evaluate Your Student's Character in relation to the character quality of **love**.

D. Familiarize Yourself With "What is Language?" Notice the Projects.

E. Review the References for "Language."

F. Notice the Answer Key.

A. Spelling Cards
Spelling Lists

Language Words
Place I - II - III

cheap	Emmanuel
communicate	enmity
importance	forever
language	head
many	heel
service	Judah
tongue	kingdom
tools	lawgiver
unselfish	**love**
weight	peace
words	Prophet
	sceptre (or er)
	seed
Bible Words	Shiloh
blessing	throne
bruise	woman

See the book *Spelling from the Scriptures* for instructions about the Spelling Cards.

B. How to Mark the Bible

1. Copy the list of Bible texts in the back of the Bible on an empty page as a guide.

2. Go to the first text in the Bible and copy the next text beside it. Go to the next one and repeat the process until they are all chain referenced.

3. Have the student present the study to family and/or friends.

4. In each student lesson there is often one or more sections that have a Bible marking study on the subject studied. (See the student's section, pages 4-5 and make your own.)

C. Evaluate Your Student's Character

This section is for the purpose of helping the teacher know how to encourage the students in becoming more **loving**. See page 7.

Place I = Grades 2-3-4
Place II = Grades 4-5-6
Place III = Grades 6-7-8

D. Familiarize Yourself With "What is Language?" – Notice the Projects

Projects

1. Practice telling the difference between literal definitions of words and spiritual or symbolic definitions of words. Express your **love** in both ways. **Love** can be expressed in a literal sense by telling your family members, "I **love** you." And **love** can be expressed in a symbolic sense by actions such as special deeds of kindness and affection for those you **love**. An example of **love** being expressed in a symbolic sense would be to pick a bouquet of flowers and give them to Grandmother with a kiss.

"My little children let us not
love in word, neither in tongue;
but in deed and in truth"
I John 3:18.

2. Fill your communications with **love**, verbal and non-verbal. (Example: when father or mother says, "Would you please wash the dishes?" quickly answer, "Yes, I will be happy to do them.")

3. Use a bowl and fill it with written ideas of kind acts such as: for the next hour, smile when someone is talking to you, or play with baby brother for 1/2 hour, or offer to do dishes for your sister today. Place the bowl on the dining room table. For any communication other than a **loving** one the offender must draw a communication of **love** out of the bowl and do what it says (carry out no more than two weeks). The purpose of this is to help members of the family to be aware of their attitudes and actions.

E. Review the References for "Language"

Teacher, read through this section before working on the lesson with the student.

See pages 8.

F. Notice the Answer Key

The Answer Key for the student book is found on page 12.

Step 3

Read the Lesson Aim.

Lesson Aim

This lesson is an introduction to Language. It will teach the child the character quality of **love** through "God With Us."

The **love** of God is the first duty of man, and this springs from just views of His attributes or excellencies of character which afford the highest delight to the sanctified heart. Esteem and reverence constitute ingredients in this affection, and a fear of offending Him is its inseparable effect.

In the beginning God communicated face to face with man. Man sinned and could no longer have open communion with God. To solve this problem, so God would not be misunderstood, Jesus became flesh (the Word) and dwelt among men. He would be an example of **love** to draw men back to God and the language of heaven.

Language helps us communicate with each other. Genesis 11:1 says, *"And the whole earth was of one language, and of one speech."* But when sin changed things then the people on earth were separated by many different languages.

Communicating gives us understanding. God longed to communicate with the sinful people on Earth. He sent the best "Word" from Heaven to explain **love**. Since language is the communication of thoughts and feeling and since a person's thoughts and feelings make up his moral character, than a person's language is an index to their moral character. God's character is revealed through His Word—the Bible, and through Jesus Christ who is also called the Word of God.

Jesus was God's best communication of **love** in the language of heaven. This example will be studied throughout eternity.

Step 4

Prepare to begin the Language Lesson.

To Begin the Language Lesson

Play a game of children's Scrabble or a similar type of game (without the competition).

Step 5

Begin the Language lesson. Cover only what can be understood by your student. Make the lessons a family project by all being involved in part or all of the lesson. These lessons are designed for the whole family.

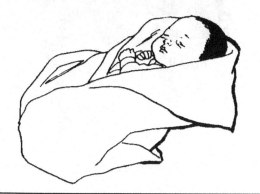

Steps in Bible Study

1. Prayer

2. Read the verses/meditate/memorize.

3. Look up key words in *Strong's Concordance* and find their meaning in the Hebrew or Greek dictionary in the back of that book.

4. Cross reference (marginal reference) with other Bible texts. An excellent study tool is *The Treasury of Scripture Knowledge.*

5. Use Bible custom books for more information on the times.

6. Write a summary of what you have learned from those verses.

7. Mark key thoughts in the margin of your Bible.

8. Share your study with others to reinforce the lessons you have learned.

Review Questions

1. What were the circumstances under which the first promise of a Redeemer was given? (Genesis 3:14-15)

2. What promise was made to Abraham, and what did it mean? (Genesis 12:1-3; Galatians 3:16)

3. Through what tribe of Israel was the Messiah to come? (Genesis 49:10)

4. What promise was given through Moses? (Deuteronomy 18:17-19)

5. Through whom was the permanence of David's kingdom assured? (II Samuel 7:12-17; Ezekiel 21:25-27; Luke 1:32)

6. What exalted ideas concerning the Messiah were made prominent? (Isaiah 9:6, 7; Psalm 45:1-8; 72:1-11)

7. What also was foretold of His relation to sin? (Isaiah 53; Zechariah 12:10)

8. What is the significance of the name which John applies to Christ? (John 14:9; Matthew 1:23)

9. What important facts are stated of Him in John 1:1-4
   a.
   b.
   c.

10. As part of the great scheme of human redemption, what did the Word become? What is the meaning of the words *"became flesh?"* (Matthew 1:23)

Notes

Children need **love**.

Evaluating Your Child's Character

Check the appropriate box for your student's level of development,
or your own, as the case may be.

Maturing Nicely (MN), Needs Improvement (NI), Poorly Developed (PD), Absent (A)

Love

1. *"**Charity** suffereth long and is kind"* (I Corinthians 13:4). Does my child show a maturity of **love** that enables them to be kind while suffering from hunger, tiredness, or discomfort?

MN NI PD A
❑   ❑   ❑   ❑

2. When the child encounters people with character deficiencies, is the child's reaction one of **loving** pity and concern instead of condemnation?

MN NI PD A
❑   ❑   ❑   ❑

3. Does your child seem to **love** God more as a result of studying the material contained in the Bible?

MN NI PD A
❑   ❑   ❑   ❑

4. *"**Charity**...vaunteth not itself; is not puffed up."* Does the child refrain from comparing himself with others? Do they make comments like "I can read better than _____ ."

MN NI PD A
❑   ❑   ❑   ❑

5. *"**Charity**...seeketh not her own."* Is the child willing for others to have the best or the most of desirable things?

MN NI PD A
❑   ❑   ❑   ❑

6. *"**Love** your enemies."* Does the child initiate reconciliation with or do kind things for those who have hard feelings toward him or who have treated him unfairly?

MN NI PD A
❑   ❑   ❑   ❑

7. *"**Love** covers a multitude of sins."* Is the child eager to tell you about the failures of others or do they **lovingly** shield others from exposure where possible to do so with integrity?

MN NI PD A
❑   ❑   ❑   ❑

8. *"**Charity**...thinketh no evil."* Is the child unsuspecting, ever placing the most favorable construction upon the motives and acts of others?

MN NI PD A
❑   ❑   ❑   ❑

References

Language

Counsels to Teachers 216 – "One of the fundamental branches of learning is language study. In all our schools special care should be taken to teach the students to use the English language correctly in speaking, reading, and writing. Too much cannot be said in regard to the importance of thoroughness in these lines. One of the most essential qualifications of a teacher is the ability to speak and read distinctly and forcibly. He who knows how to use the English language fluently and correctly can exert a far greater influence than one who is unable to express his thoughts readily and clearly."

Counsels to Teachers 215 – "Many who feel that they have finished their education are faulty in spelling and in writing, and can neither read nor speak correctly. Not a few who study the classics and other higher branches of learning, and who reach certain standards, finally fail because they have neglected to do thorough work in the common branches. They have never obtained a good knowledge of the English language. They need to go back and begin to climb from the first round of the ladder."

Education 234-235 – "And in every branch of education there are objects to be gained more important than those secured by mere technical knowledge. Take language, for example. More important than the acquirement of foreign languages, living or dead, is the ability to write and speak one's mother tongue with ease and accuracy; but no training gained through a knowledge of grammatical rules can compare in importance with the study of language from a higher point of view. With this study, to a great degree, is bound up life's weal or woe.

"The chief requisite of language is that it be pure and kind and true—'the outward expression of an inward grace.' God says: *'Whatsoever things are true, whatsoever things are honest, whatsoever things are just, whatsoever things are pure, whatsoever things are lovely, whatsoever things are of good report; if there be any virtue, and if there be any praise, think on these things'* (Philippians 4:8). And if such are the thoughts, such will be the expression."

Christ's Object Lessons 336 – "Every Christian is called to make known to others the unsearchable riches of Christ; therefore, he should seek for perfection in speech. He should present the word of God in a way that will commend it to the hearers. God does not design that His human channels shall be uncouth. It is not His will that man shall belittle or degrade the heavenly current that flows through him to the world....We should accustom ourselves to speak in pleasant tones, to use pure and correct language, and words that are kind and courteous."

Evangelism 668 – "The teachers in our schools should not tolerate in the students ungainly attitudes and uncouth gestures, wrong intonations in reading, or incorrect accents or emphasis. Perfection of speech and voice should be urged upon every student."

Counsels to Teachers 217 – "Unless we can clothe our ideas in appropriate language, of what avail is our education?"

Counsels to Teachers 243 – "God has given us the gift of speech that we may recite to others His dealing with us, that His love and compassion may touch other hearts, and

that praise may arise from other souls also to Him who has called them out of darkness into His marvelous light."

6 Testimonies 337 – "Of all the gifts that God has bestowed upon men, none is more precious than the gift of speech. If sanctified by the Holy Spirit, it is a power for good. It is with the tongue that we convince and persuade; with it we offer prayer and praise to God; and with it we convey rich thoughts of the Redeemer's **love**."

Counsels to Teachers 156-157 – "He will help you to use the talent of speech in so Christ like a way that peace and **love** will reign in the home."

Sons and Daughters of God 72 – "It is our privilege to grow more and more like Him every day. Then we shall acquire the power to express our **love** for Him in higher, purer speech, and our ideas will enlarge and deepen, and our judgment become more sound and trustworthy, while our testimony will have more of life and assurance. We are not to cultivate the language of the earthy and be so familiar with the conversation of men, that the language of Canaan will be new and unfamiliar to us...The Scripture says of Christ that grace was poured into His lips, that He might *know how to speak a* *word in season to him that is weary.'* And the Lord bids us, *'Let your speech be always with grace,'* *'that it may minister grace unto the hearers.'* When the heart is pure, rich treasure of wisdom will flow forth."

6 Testimonies 380 – "Knowledge will be of little advantage to us unless we cultivate the talent of speech; but it is a wonderful power when combined with the ability to speak wise, helpful words, and to speak them in a way that will command attention...The truth must not be marred by being communicated through defective utterance."

1 Testimonies 216 – "But while we are commanded to separate from the world, it is not necessary that we become coarse and rough, and descend to common expression, and make our remarks as rude as possible. The truth is designed to elevate the receiver, to refine his taste and sanctify his judgment. There should be a continual effort to imitate the society we expect soon to join; namely, angels of God who have never fallen by sin. The character should be holy, the manners comely, the words without guile, and thus should we follow on step by step until we are fitted for translation."

Fundamentals of Christian Education 130 – "[In the Bible] The truth is clothed in elevated language, which exerts a fascinating power over the mind; the thought is lifted up from the things of earth, and brought to contemplate the glory of the future immortal life."

Counsels to Teachers 238 – "He should endeavor to use correct language. There is a large class who are careless in the way they speak, yet by careful, painstaking attention these may become representatives of the truth. Every day they should make advancement. They should not detract from their usefulness and influence by cherishing defects of manner, tone, or language. Common, cheap expressions should be replaced by sound, pure words...We should be careful not to give an incorrect pronunciation of our words. There are men among us who in theory know better than to use incorrect language, yet who in practice make frequent mistakes. The Lord would have us careful to do our best, making wise use of our faculties and opportunities. He has endowed men with gifts with which to bless and edify others; it is our duty so to educate ourselves that we may be fitted for the great work committed to us."

The Desire of Ages 34 – "Through nature, through types and symbols, through patriarchs and prophets, God had spoken to the world. Lessons must be given to humanity in the language of humanity.

6 Testimonies 322 – "The human agent will learn how to represent the divine Companion with whom he is associated...They will be gifted with power to clothe the message of truth with a sacred beauty."

"The Scripture says of Christ that grace was poured into His lips, that He might *'know how to speak a word in season to him that is weary.'* "

Answer Key

Page 6

1-3 Teacher, check.

4. One

5. Teacher, check.

Page 7-8

Teacher, check.

Page 9

1. Symbol

2. Language

3. One

4. See Genesis 11:1-9.

5. Sentence

6. **Love**

7. Selfish

8. **Love**

9. Height, depth

10. See page 5.

Page 9 continued

11. See page 5.

Page 15

1. Study, approved

2. Wrong pronunciation, misspelled words, improper punctuation and sentence structure

4. Words are like seeds that some-day, will have a harvest.

5. See the list of spelling words on page 2 in the Teacher's Section.

Page 17

1. Study

2. Wrong pronunciation, misspelled words, improper punctuation and sentence structure

3. Chaff

4. Seeds

5. See the list of spelling words on page 2 in the Teacher's Section.

Gardening Sheet

Lesson __One__   Subject __Language__

Title __"What is Language?"__

In Season	Out of Season
(This can be for both "In Season" and "Out of Season.")	corm
	fertilizer
	fungicide
	grafting
What is garden language? Learn the terms of the garden. Some to start with are:	greenhouse
	hotbeds
	insects
	lawn
companion planting	mulch
seeds	peat moss
seedlings	pollen
analyzing	pruning
soil	tuber
planting	landscape
transplanting	flower
fertilizing	fruit
disease	grass
pests	herb
weeds	nut
mulching	plant
supports	shrub
annuals	tree
biennials	vegetable
perennials	
bulbs	(If you think of other garden words add them to this list. Learn about the words you do not understand.)
compost	
cold frame	

Student
Section

"O many a shaft, at random sent,
Finds mark the archer little meant,
And many a word at random spoken
May soothe or wound a heart that's broken."
    —Sir Walter Scott

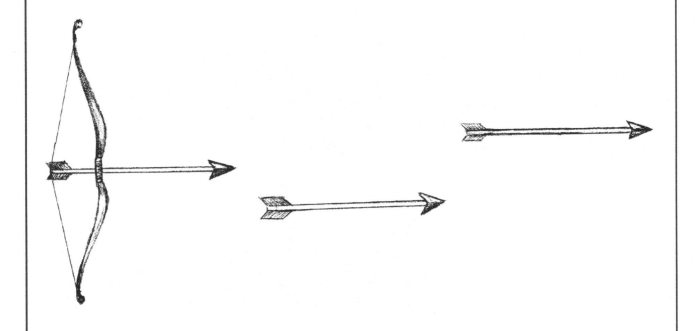

What is Language?

Research

"Let the <u>word</u> of Christ dwell in you richly in all wisdom...."
Colossians 3:16

Words

Words are signs or symbols of ideas. In itself a word may not express a complete thought. To make a complete thought, a word is joined with others in a combination called a sentence. An example would be *"His name shall be called Immanuel, God with us."* All the words used by a large group or race of people to express their thoughts, and to communicate with one another, are called a language. We use the English language.

In the time of our Bible lesson the Greek language was the common language.

"Our little world is the lesson book of the universe."
The Desire of Ages 19

The Beginning

"And the whole earth was of one language, and of one speech."
Genesis 11:1

In the beginning God talked with man face to face. But when man sinned he lost the privilege of open communion with God. No longer could he enjoy *"the voice* [to call aloud—sound] *of the Lord God walking in the garden in the cool of the day"* (Genesis 3:8).

Adam left the Garden of Eden and, in the years that followed, his descendants increased. *"And the whole earth was of one language, and of one speech"* up until the time when the tower of Babel was built (Genesis 11:1). *"And the Lord came down to see the city and the tower, which the children of men builded.*

"And the Lord said, Behold, the people is one, and they have all one language; and this they begin to do: and now nothing will be restrained from them, which they have imagined to do.

"Go to, let us go down, and there confound their language, that they may not understand one another's speech.

"So the Lord scattered them abroad across the face of all the earth: and they left off to build the city" (Genesis 11:5-8).

This story shows us some important things. When the people could no longer understand one another's speech, they could not go on planning and working together.

Every man thinks alone inside himself. Unless he shares his ideas in some way, no one else can know them. In order for thought and knowledge to be shared, there must be language. Just like a person cannot live without breathing, so a society cannot exist without language.

The society of heaven is able to work together because they all understand the language of **love**. God wants us to learn heaven's language here so we can all work together now and throughout eternity.

God wants us to learn heaven's language.

Reinforce
Many Languages
Place I - II
Color the picture below.

"...So the Lord scattered them abroad across the face of all the earth: and they left off to build the city."

Genesis 11:8

Language of Love

"Even as the Son of man came not to be ministered unto, but to minister, and to give his life a ransom for many."
Matthew 20:28

The language of the **love** of God, angels, and men, is sacrifice, or unselfish service. For this reason the **love** of God requires the *"form of a servant"* to express itself. In order to communicate this kind of **love** to the world, Jesus came *"not to be ministered unto, but to minister, and to give his life a ransom for many"* (Matthew 20:28). "He was the Word of God—God's thought made audible."* And the Father also has this unselfish kind of **love** for the world because *"He gave his only begotten Son"* (John 3:16).

In heaven, Satan had misrepresented God as being selfish. He falsely attributed to God the desire for self-exaltation. "With his own evil characteristics he sought to invest the **loving** Creator. Thus he deceived angels. Thus he deceived men."

"The Exercise of Force Is Contrary To The Principles of God's Government..."

"That the gloomy shadows might be lightened, that the world might be brought back to God, Satan's deceptive power was to be broken. This could not be done by force. The exercise of force is contrary to the principles of God's government; He desires only the service of **love**; and **love** cannot be commanded; it cannot be won by force or authority. Only by **love** is **love** awakened. To know God is to **love** Him; His character must be manifested in contrast to the character of Satan. This work only one being in all the universe could do. Only He who knew the height and depth of the **love** of God could make it known. Upon the world's dark night the *'Sun of Righteousness'* must rise, *'with healing in his wings'* (Malachi 4:2)."*

Unselfish, loving ministry is the language of heaven.

*The Desire of Ages 19, 22

Jesus was God's best communication of **love** in the language of heaven. This example will be studied throughout eternity. In the meantime, while Jesus is physically in heaven, He desires you to speak the word of **love** for Him. In a special sense you are now to be God's **love** letter, and *"epistle...known and read of all men"* (II Corinthians 3:2). It is for this reason that we are going to study the subject of language. We want to be able to communicate God's precious **love** to others in as perfect and attractive a way as possible. After all, "lessons must be given to humanity in the language of humanity."*

It is not God's will that man shall belittle or degrade the heavenly current that flows through him to the world. Rather, He longs to give us the power to clothe the message of His **love** with sacred beauty. If it is your heart's desire to cooperate with God in this mission, here is a powerful promise from His Word which you may prayerfully claim:

"I thank my God always on your behalf, for the grace of God which is given you by Jesus Christ; That in everything ye are enriched by him, in all utterance and in all knowledge" (I Corinthians 1:4-5).

Reflect

Letters = A word _ _ _ _ _ _ _ _   L̲   O̲   V̲   E̲

Words = Sentences _ _ _ _ _ _   God is l̲o̲v̲e̲.

Sentences = Paragraphs _ _ _ _   "For God so l̲o̲v̲e̲d̲ the world, that He gave His only begotten Son, that whosoever believeth in Him should not perish, but have everlasting life."

Paragraphs = Chapters _ _ _ _   Matthew, Mark, Luke, John

Chapters = A Book _ _ _ _ _ _   The Bible is a Book.

*The Desire of Ages 34

Review

Place I

1. Copy this word in the heart. (LOVE)

2. Copy this sentence below. (God is **love**.)

3. Trace these letters as you read these sentences.

LETTERS MAKE UP A WORD. WORDS MAKE UP A SENTENCE.

4. There was _____ language in the beginning on the earth.

5. Draw the story about the tower of Babel on the next page showing how many languages came to be used on this earth.

The Tower of Babel

Read Genesis 11:1-9.

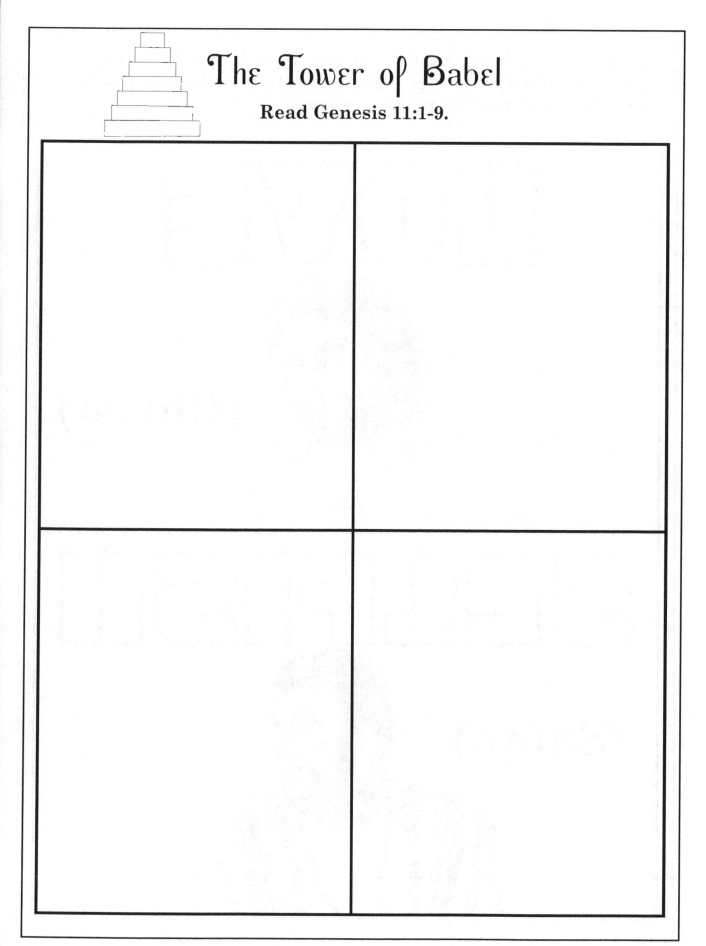

6. Color the word **love** pink (the color pink is made up of white and red - white = purity and red = blood - Christ shed His blood for you). Color the word <u>selfish</u> black (black can represent sin).

LOVE

(Christ)

SELFISH

(Satan)

Review
Place II - III

1. A word is a sign or __ __ __ __ __ __ .

2. The words used by a large group of people or race to express their thoughts are called a _____ .

3. How many languages were there at first on the earth? _____

4. When and how did more languages arise? _____

5. Words join together to form a __ __ __ __ __ __ __ __ __ .

6. What is the language of heaven? _____

7. Satan says that God is _____ .

8. Only by _____ is **love** awakened.

9. Only Christ who knew the _____ and _____ of the **love** of God could make it known.

10. Since Jesus has gone back to heaven, how can His **love** be made known? _____
_____

11. How does the study of language fit in with showing God's **love**?
_____
_____
_____

"So the Lord scattered them abroad from thence upon the face of all the earth...."

Genesis 11:8

Reinforce
Place II - III

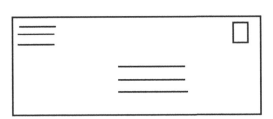

1. Be a **love** letter from God. (For example: Send a **love** letter to Grandma or Grandpa, etc. and tell them now much you and God **love** them. Do the best job you can, making it neat and using correct language, and spelling.

2. Sing the hymn, "If Any Little Word of Mine." Put into practice what these words talk about.

"If any little word of mine May make a dark life brighter, If any little song of mine May make a sad heart lighter,

"God help me speak the helping word, And sweeten it with singing, And drop it in some lonely vale, To set the echoes ringing."

Research

Powerful Words

Since words are the signs of ideas, you would think that the use of words is generally controlled by the ideas. But this is not always the case. Frequently thoughts and ideas are born of words. This is one of the main reasons why we should be so guarded in what words we choose in speaking or writing. Words have the power to react on our own minds as well as the minds of other people. Once you express something in words, your mind will tend to see it that way in the future, even if what was said was wrong! We cannot erase the impressions that have been made on our brains by our words.

The Weight of Words

Words may be empty and foolish, as light and frothy as the windswept foam. Words of this kind speak of empty minds and shallow thoughts. Words may also be weighty and full of meaning. **Loving** words are "the outward expression of an inward grace."

Words are very powerful. A mere word has been known to change the course of nations. And who has not known someone whose heart has been broken by a simple word? But, on the brighter side, a little word of **love** has the power to encourage the despairing, bring joy to the sad, sweeten some bitter cup, and gladden a life.

A Word

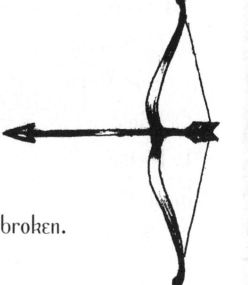

Oh many a shaft, at random sent,

Finds mark the archer little meant,

And many a word at random spoken

May soothe or wound a heart that's broken.

—Sir Walter Scott

Importance of Words

"So be ye holy in all manner of conversation."

I Peter 1:15

The wisest man of earth once said, *"A word fitly spoken is like apples of gold in pictures* [baskets] *of silver"* (Proverbs 25:11). And a wiser than he has solemnly told us, *"Every idle word that men shall speak, they shall give account thereof in the day of judgment. For by thy words thou shalt be justified, and by thy words thou shalt be condemned"* (Matthew 12:36).

How important, then, are our words! *"So be ye holy in all manner of conversation"* (I Peter 1:15).

Tools

It has been said that man is a tool-using creature, and that his strength lies in the tools he uses. Among these tools, if carefully selected, words are most helpful. But, sad to say, many men do not have access to these tools because they do not study. The world is full of poets who are silent because they cannot put into words what they feel, and of great thinkers whose ideas would make them famous if they only were masters of the use of words.

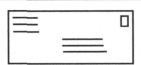

Read the poem, "A Word," and the story "A Love Letter from God." (See pages 19-20.)

"A Word
Fitly Spoken
Is Like Apples
Of Gold
In Pictures
[baskets]
Of Silver."

Color the apples red and the basket silver.

Study

"Study to show thyself
approved unto God
a workman that needeth not
to be ashamed."
II Timothy 2:15

It mars the work, God desires to do through us and lessens our influence for good in the world if we use incorrect or poorly pronounced words in speaking, misspelled words, improper punctuation, capitalization, or sentence structure in writing.

"Study to show thyself approved unto God." A person must study if they are to become knowledgeable; and the person who does not want to apply himself sufficiently to show himself *"approved unto God,"* will fail of ever becoming *"a workman that needeth not to be ashamed"* (II Timothy 2:15).

Avoid Cheapness

The effort you make in study will not only teach you how to write and speak well, but it will also have an influence on your soul, even under the most trying circumstances, to never use the wrong word.

Beware of falling into the all-too-common habit of being cheap in your language. It is very easy to be cheap. To use slang expressions requires no effort. All one needs to do is loose the tongue and let himself go. To be sure, he who is lazy and careless in his words will find plenty of company. He may even find some admirers. But soon all the coarse chaff will be burned up. Only the good seed will endure.

He who is lazy and careless
in his words
will find plenty of company.

Sow Loving Words

They reach the richest harvest of good deeds,
Who sow but <u>loving</u> words, most precious seeds.

To be cheap in language is to make life nothing but a round of existence, purposeless and useless. The Christian, however, will *"bridle"* his tongue and thus fulfill his glorious destiny of speaking for God. He is part of *"an holy priesthood to offer up spiritual sacrifices <u>acceptable</u> to God by Jesus Christ"* (I Peter 2:5).

"Let the words of my mouth...be <u>acceptable</u> in thy sight, O Lord" (Psalm 19:14).

The Christian cherishes the blessed hope—

• of entering into the presence of the King of kings;

• of associating with the pure, unfallen beings of heaven and other worlds;

• of talking with Jesus Christ, the great Author of perfect language and speech.

Therefore, he will view anything short of the highest excellence in language as unworthy of his calling.

May the God of all grace *"make you perfect in every good work"* (Hebrews 13:21).

"If any man offend not in word, the same is a perfect man."

James 3:2

Review
Place I

1. Finish this verse by filling in the missing words. "_____ to show

thyself _____ unto God" (II Timothy 2:15).

2. What 3 things mar our language?

    (1) _____

    (2) _____

    (3) _____

3. Pray for God to help you have pure, **loving** speech.

4. Explain the pictures on the next page to your teacher, then color the pictures. Remember words are like seeds.

5. Have your teacher dictate the spelling words. Give an oral sentence using the word.

_____

_____

_____

_____

1.

2.

3.

4.

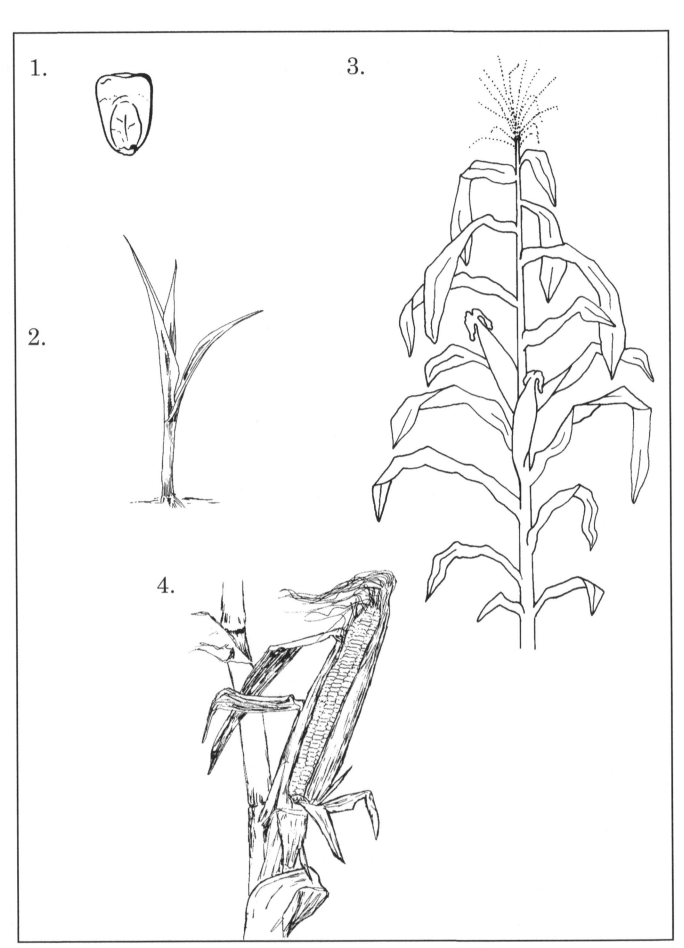

Review
Place II - III

1. Many men do not have word tools because they do not __ __ __ __ __ .

_____

_____

2. Name three things that mar a person's language. _____

_____

_____

_____

_____

3. Slang and cheap language remind us of the __ __ __ __ __ that will be burned up.

_____

_____

4. **Loving** words can be compared to good __ __ __ __ __ .

_____

_____

5. Have your teacher dictate the spelling words. Spell each word, give the spiritual and literal definition, then write a sentence using each word as relating to your Bible lesson.

_____

_____

_____

_____

_____

_____

_____

_____

_____

Reinforce

Place I - II - III

1. As a family, try communicating without using written or spoken language for a few hours. What things did you notice that you were unable to do without your word tools?_____

_____

_____

2. While you are working in the garden, let it remind you to weed out all "baby talk," "cute" expressions, and slang from your language. Help one another as a family to find good substitutes for these words or phrases.

3. Read "Creative Words," and the poem, "The Alphabet."

Creative Words

Language is made up of words. Why does man use language? He uses it because he is made in the image of God, and God Himself uses words. *"In the beginning was the Word...and the Word was God"* (John 1:1). *"By the word of the Lord were the heavens made..."* (Psalm 33:6). The creative power of God's word reminds us that the language we use can also be creative. By our choice of words we shape our own character and influence the lives of others for time and eternity. Therefore, *"If any man speak, let him speak as the oracles of God...that God in all things may be glorified through Jesus Christ, to whom be praise and dominion for ever and ever. Amen"* (I Peter 4:11).

A Word

A cheery word by a sad heart heard
    Rent the wild, wild tempest cloud.
A laughing word brought the sunshine home,
    Where the wind was roaring loud.

Twas but a sunny word of **love**,
    But the blue sky beamed again,
And over the fields of a weeping heart,
    The cloverheads sparkled then.

A word may curse, a word may bless,
    And the bosom deep is stirred
In an instant, as by an arrow shot,
    By a sharp, unkindly word.

O guard your lips! for the seed once sown
    Cannot be brought back again,
But over the fields will the harvests grow—
    In the fields of the hearts of men.

—Adapted from *B.F.M. Sours*

"A Love Letter from God"

"Upon all things in earth, and air, and sky,
He wrote the message of the Father's love."
The Desire of Ages 20

"A few days ago a little girl sent a box of spring wild flowers to me. There was not writing in the box; at least you might have said there was no writing in it; but as I opened the little box, and looked at the dainty blossoms, I found a dear little letter. Here are a few words from what I read—

"I love you, Elder Warren. I gathered these flowers for you. I think of you, and want you to be happy. I am taking the time and pains to send these to you, to remind you that I love you."

Don't you think that was a sweet little letter? But that is not all. When I had looked a little more carefully, I read something more from Someone else. Here are a few of the words—

"I love you, Luther Warren. I planted these flowers for you. I made them grow. I painted their beautiful colors. I put the perfume in them. I love you, and desire to make you happy. These blossoms are to remind you that I am thinking of you. I am getting a place ready for you, where the flowers will never fade. I want you to be ready to come and live with Me. And I also put into the heart of that little girl to send these flowers to you. Her love is My gift to you also. When I was in the world, My heart was cheered with the love of little children. I know what will cheer and encourage you. I am always thinking and planning for you, because I love you."

Oh don't you think that was the sweetest kind of a love letter?

Now, dear boys and girls, open your eyes, and look around you. See if you can find some love letters from God to you. Try to make out all the words.

You like to get letters, don't you? Do you know how to answer God's letters?"

—*Luther Warren*

The Alphabet

"But the Comforter,
which is the Holy Ghost,
whom the Father will send in my name,
he shall teach you all things."

John 14:26

At the door, behold a Teacher, asking you to come;

Be instructed, in the language, of His heavenly home;

Come, while the list is writing, have your names enrolled;

During a brief space He lingers, soon He'll shut the fold.

Every child may learn His lessons, if he perseveres.

Faith, repentance, the first letters, dotted with a tear;

Goodness, kindness, meekness, patience, gentleness and **love**,

Help to complete the <u>alphabet</u>, taught by the Heavenly Dove;

Innocence, obedience, humility and truth,

Justice, honesty, submission, must be learned by youth;

Know ye not examination day is hast'ning on?

Learn, if you would hear the Judge pronounce your task *"well done."*

Mercy lingers in the holiest, o'er the broken law,

Night and day she pleads for learners, soon she will withdraw.

Oh! before she leaves her station, learn to walk with God,

Pure and holy all who enter that bright, blest abode.

Query not about your duty—duty's path is plain,

Repent of sin, believe in Jesus, live no more invain.

Satan would be glad to have you think you are too young,

To obtain such wondrous knowledge, and a fadeless crown.

Unto every one that asketh, wisdom shall be given,

Would you seek that realm to enter where is cloudless light?

Xercise the Christian graces, keep your armor bright.

Yet a little He that cometh, will not tarry more;

Zealous for His Father's glory, He'll all things restore.

—Adapted M M Osgood

Reinforce

Find A Name

**See if you can find a person's name in the Bible
which starts with each of the letters in the alphabet.
Use a separate piece of paper.
Circle the letters below as you find each name.**

A B C D E F G

H I J K L M N

O P Q R S T U

V W X Y Z

Outline of School Program

Age	Grade	Program
Birth through Age 7	Babies Kindergarten and Pre-school	*Family Bible Lessons* (This includes: Bible, Science–Nature, and Character)
Age 8	First Grade	*Family Bible Lessons* (This includes: Bible, Science–Nature, and Character) + Language Program (*Writing and Spelling Road to Reading and Thinking* [WSRRT])
Age 9-14 or 15	Second through Eighth Grade	*The Desire of all Nations* (This includes: Health, Mathematics, Music, Science–Nature, History/Geography/Prophecy, Language, and Voice–Speech) + Continue using WSRRT
Ages 15 or 16-19	Ninth through Twelfth Grade	9 – *Cross and Its Shadow I** + Appropriate Academic Books 10 – *Cross and Its Shadow II** + Appropriate Academic Books 11 – *Daniel the Prophet** + Appropriate Academic Books 12 – *The Seer of Patmos** (Revelation) + Appropriate Academic Books *or you could continue using *The Desire of Ages*
Ages 20-25	College	Apprenticeship

Made in the USA
Las Vegas, NV
17 September 2021